I0488652

Contents

Disclaimer

Your Free Gift

As a way of saying *thanks* for purchasing and reading this book, I am giving you a free gift and I invite you to take a look at my blog – http://entrepreneurenhanced.com

To get this gift click on the photo or click on the blog to sign up to my email list.

You will receive $0.99 offers, free content, tips and even free books.

#1 - Consistent Action

Spring doesn't come with one flower or a flower doesn't bring you spring. The same principle goes with self-publishing and with any other kind of business, whether it's offline or online. To succeed and to make profits, you need to work on a daily basis (every single day with occasional break-offs), so put your butt to work. Take a break once you finish a book or a project.

The only effective way to do this properly is to force yourself for at least 30 days to write, research and learn new things on a daily basis until it becomes a habit. Here's what you need to do:

1. Set an hour at which you write every day - try doing it in the morning.

2. Write at least 2,000 words every day, even if you're writing nonsense - after you read your first drafts, you will edit them and probably have more ideas.

3. Repeat this process at least 30 days until it becomes a habit.

I usually write around 15,000 to 40,000 words a month and this includes blog posts, drafts, comments, and books. My books are usually between 6,000 to 18,000 words (5,000 - 6,000 words - FREE; 6,000 - 8,000 words - $0.99; 9,000 - 15,000 words - $2.99; 16,000 - 20,000 words - $3.99).

#2 - Email List

"The money is in the list" is something what online gurus, entrepreneurs and marketers claim. I wasn't convinced about it until I've studied the case and I built one of my own. An email list is one of the most powerful assets and it comes with several advantages:

1. It's yours - you don't depend on anybody, you don't depend on a platform, it's absolutely yours.

2. You can promote any kind of product (related to your niche) you want.

3. You don't have any limits related to its size.

4. You can start building it fast.

5. It's profitable and relatively cheap to maintain.

An email list generally requires a blog or a website and the best way to grow it is to offer your audience an eBook or a course (a lead magnet). Kindle Publishing is a great way to build an email list by using your books (like I do) - at the end or at the beginning of each book, make sure to include a lead magnet your audience.

To boost the submissions, make sure to run promotions from time to time and also consider creating a perma-free book (more about this later). As a self-publisher, you can launch your books (free or at $0.99) by using your email list and the results can be quite amazing. I know a few people who have huge lists of over 100,000 subscribers and when they launch their books, they're making over 1,000 units priced at $0.99. By doing that, your ranking and visibility explodes and then you will start making organic sales at full price ($2.99 or more).

#3 - Put Keywords in the title

The title of a book has a huge influence upon your book. A title doesn't necessarily have to sound great, it sometimes just needs to have the right keywords and the right Keyword Ratio (if your title has 4 words and the keyword has 2 words, your keyword ratio is 50% - a higher keyword ratio will rank your books higher in Amazon's search bar). The best 2 tools to make keyword research are:

1. Google Keyword Planner - see how many searches a month that keyword makes

2. Amazon's search bar - see what people are looking for based on the number of recent searches

Keywords are not only important in the title, they're also important when you use them in your subtitles and when you upload the book (you can use up to 5 keywords for CreateSpace and up to 7 keywords for KDP). Before uploading your book or before you create your cover, make sure that you are using the right keywords.

#4 - Create a Podcast

Podcasting is really great for boosting up your visibility. Generally, podcasts are hosted by SoundCloud (for free) and they will also be available on iTunes. What you need is an editing software and a professional microphone and you're good to go.

If you decide to start a podcast means that you will commit to releasing an episode every 1-2 weeks. By doing this, more people will discover you, your blog's traffic will increase and thus, you will have more customers and more subscribers. Makes sense?

#5 - Create a blog

A blog is a *must* for any publisher, for any online business and for any online entrepreneur, especially if you sell digital content (eBooks & eCourses). After you learn, grow and start seeing the potential of your blog, you will see that it will become your primary source of income (thanks to the traffic and email list). The mechanism is simple:

Books => Blog Traffic => subscribers

Google => Blog Traffic => subscribers

Advertising => Blog Traffic => subscribers

Social Media => Blog Traffic => subscribers

Subscribers => Money

Subscribers => More traffic

Subscribers => Launch books => Sales => Money

OR

Books + Google + Social Media => Blog Traffic => Subscribers => Money + Blog Traffic => More money

Just like an email list, your blog is your own asset and nobody can take it from you. It's quite risky to depend just on one platform (Amazon for example) - you literally depend on their rules, your income depends on their royalties. Right now they offer 35% for books priced between $0.99 - $2.99 and $9.99 - $200 and they offer 70% royalty for books priced between $2.99 and $9.99, but what if they make an overnight rule to pay everyone 50% royalty? I'll tell you what happens, your income will significantly drop with at least 20%.

A blog will help you grow, get in touch with customers/readers, you will get more exposure and people can interact with you. Not only that you can promote your books on your blog, but you can also pursue other profitable activities such as making money from ads (Google AdSense), affiliate marketing, coaching, selling courses or selling physical products. Also, your blog can be easily connected to multiple websites and platforms, including YouTube where you can start your own channel related to your niche, to your books and to the content from your blog.

It took a while until I finally created my blog - http://entrepreneurenhanced.com but I finally did it. To be honest, I had this in mind long time ago, but my budget wasn't allowing me to do it. Professional blogging for a self-publisher requires a lot of tools - email list, domain, web hosting, plugins, a theme (design), content, time, professional email (from the domain - my professional email costs $4.99/month - ryan@entrepreneurenhanced.com) and much more.

In other words, a blog is a unique asset which you need to implement.

#6 - Cross Promotion

This trick can really boost up your sales and visibility on Amazon and on any platform. At the end of each book, make sure to create a section called "Other books by this author" and write short descriptions about them of 50-100 words (no more than 100 words) and add a small thumbnail with the cover of your book. Also, add hyperlinks to Amazon (don't include affiliate links, it's against Amazon's terms of service). When people like your work and see that you have even more, they will be tempted to click to read other books on the same topic.

The cross promotion mechanism goes like this:

Book A promotes Book B, Book C and Book D

Book B promotes Book A, Book C and Book D

Book C promotes Book D, Book A and Book B

Book D promotes Book B, Book C and Book A

I would say that this is one of the simplest and effective ways of promoting your books for free. The real power behind this technique is when you promote one of the books. Let's say you get 3,000 free units during a 5 day promotion on one of the books. From those 3,000 customers, at least 10% will be curious about your other books and they will click on them. This means that at least 300 people at least another 10% will buy your other books, that will results in approximately 30 sales.

#7 - Create an Audible version

Audible ACX is an Amazon company and it allows you to create an audio version of your book. As you would guess, you need someone to narrate your book for you (a professional). Usually, the audio version of a 10,000 word book will cost you around $300 (maybe more). If you think you have a clear voice, you have experience in this field and you have the necessary tools (software, professional microphone, skills, powerful PC), then do it yourself. If you don't have any idea about this, but you still want an audio version, wait until you can afford to create it.

I highly recommend you to create an audio version of your books after you launch it an only if you sell at least 4-5 copies a day constantly. If you're selling less than this amount, then don't waste your time - you may break even over time, but you would better invest your money somewhere else.

Audible ACX allows you to create audio versions only if you're a UK or a US resident.

#8 - *Create a Paperback Version*

Creating a paperback (print) edition for your book increase your income with 20% from what you earn from what you earn on Kindle. Even if eBooks are cheaper, environmentally friendly and they get delivered a lot faster, there still are some folks out there who prefer reading a real book rather than a digital one. So what you need to do is to create print editions to fulfill those customers too.

I personally use CreateSpace and I recommend it to anyone who is self-publishing on a budget. I actually have a bargain $0.99 book which explains exactly step-by-step what to do to upload it and I also explain everything in detail - CreateSpace Publishing For Independent Self-Publishers (check the list at the end). By using a print format, your product page will give you more authority in front of other authors who don't have and people will be more likely to purchase your book.

I have 10 titles on CreateSpace so far and I am averaging 20-50 sales a month and I generate around $40 - $80 / month from them. It's not ground shattering, but I think it's decent. Creating and formatting a cover for Createspace isn't expensive, I use a gig from Fiverr which charges me only $15 - front, back, spine + stock photo included.

CreateSpace pays after 30 days - if you make $50 in January, you get paid on 29th February.

#9 - Create a Lead Magnet

A lead magnet is a way to grab your customers' attention and take their email list. Every email list that you see on the web or any successful business that you see have in common one thing - a leading magnet.

The mechanism is simple - you give them something for free (video, course or ebook) in exchange for their email.

I personally joined a lot of them and sometimes I feel like it's worth to purchase their entry-level offer or even more. I have a personal idol from whom I bought all his books, courses and everything he sells. Not everything I purchased was 100% helpful, but at least 80% was worth my time and money.

#10 - Pay for advertising

If you just entered the world of online self-publishing, then you might want to consider paying a few websites to promote your books.

Hey, I've been there too. It's really hard at the beginning, especially if you don't have any experience with online marketing, blogging, SEO, social media marketing, etc. I've started from zero, just like many others and by working on a daily basis and studying. I really got to a point where I am making enough money to support my personal expenses. It's hard when you don't know where to look, where to invest and what to trust.

At the beginning you should really invest at least $100 for every book that you launch - there are a few websites which can boost up everything, whether you're promoting your book for free or at $0.99. Here's a short list of places where you can promote your book:

- *BooksButterfly*
- *BKnights (Fiverr gig)*
- *eBookshabit*
- *Reading Deals*

- *Read Cheaply*
- *BookSends*
- *BargainBooksy*
- *BookGorilla*
- *Genre Pulse*
- *BookBub (this one is hard to get)*
- *EreaderNewsToday*

I've tried all them and the best so far from that list are BooksButterfly, EreaderNewsToday and BKnights. Be careful if you want to invest your money somewhere else, some websites are scams - eReadergirl charged me $20 and told me that they forgot to run my ad and they didn't send me a refund.

#11 - Enroll in KDP Select

Amazon's exclusive program is something which you seriously need to consider, especially if you don't have any background in the self-publishing field. 80% of my books are enrolled in KDP Select (except my perma-free books, my premium discounted bundle and my $0.99 books). Here are the benefits of enrolling in KDP Select:

1. Access to Kindle Unlimited - people can borrow your book and you will be paid for each individual read page. While people will borrow your book, your title will rank higher in Amazon's searches.

2. 70% royalty on the other stores - some international Amazon stores (Amazon.com.au, Amazon.nl, etc.) won't give you the highest royalty unless you choose this option.

3. Promote your book - this is the main reason why I enroll most of my books in this program. You have 2 ways to promote your books

- *Free promotion days - you can give away your book for free for up to 5 days consecutively and your book will gain more visibility. The more free downloads, the higher you rank. Typically, every 10 free units are equivalent to 1 paid unit in visibility.*
- *Countdown deals - you can promote your books (priced between $2.99 and $24.99) up to 7 days at $0.99 or more ($1.99, $2.99, etc.) and during the promotion you still get 70% royalty (even at $0.99). Countdown deals can be applied only after you keep your book enrolled in KDP Select for at least 30 days and*

without changing the price for 30 days.

Note that when you enroll in KDP Select you are not allowed to share your book anywhere else outside Amazon for 90 days.

#12 - Write in the morning

Time is limited, so use it wisely. To make sure that you're working/writing every day you will need to set a fixed hour when to do it. I usually write whenever I have time, but I always make sure to write in the morning.

Waking up at 7:00 AM comes with a lot of benefits - going for a short jog (15 minutes), starting to write for 2 hours and managing emails and other online activities. So, in this way, until 11:00 AM, you've done a lot of great things for yourself. If you hate waking up early, just think that if you don't do it now for yourself, maybe you will do it for someone else (or you're already doing it).

#13 - Bundle books

If you've written a series of books or multiple on the same topic (at least 4), then you might consider to bundle them together and create a premium offer (no lending, no Kindle Unlimited, no borrowing). If a book costs $2.99 and you have 5 books, offer them at a 50% discount - instead of pricing them at $14.99, price them at $6.99 or $7.99.

By doing this you have multiple advantages:

- *You enhance visibility*
- *You create a great offer for your customers*
- *You make more money from just 1 purchase ($4 royalty)*
- *People who see your bundle probably want just 1 book and they will buy it individually (more exposure)*

My bundle will come out really soon at a 50% discount (probably in January or February 2016) related to self-publishing, online marketing and productivity.

#14 - Invest in a good cover

People tend to judge a book by its cover. While I love to acquire a high quality cover, I don't like spending exaggerating amounts of money on them (like over $300). A good looking cover should include the following things:

- Premium stock photo (related to your topic/niche)
- Cartoonish design
- Eye catching colors (blue, green, red, blue)
- Details to enhance its overall look

I usually pay from $30 to $50 for a cover and it includes paperback formatting (for CreateSpace), front, back and spine design and it also includes a stock photo. They're not the best covers in the world, but at least they're clean and decent. When I will be reaching $5K or $10K a month, I will probably consider investing $300 in every book cover.

But let's face it, $300 for a single cover is kind of too much.

#15 - Edit your book

There's no such thing as perfection and thus, there's no such thing as a perfect book, but we can do several things to enhance the user experience and its overall quality. Editing a book refers to multiple processes:

- *Properly formatting for Kindle devices (adequate spacing, fonts, page size etc.)*
- *Proofreading*
- *Re-writing phrases which don't make sense (I often do that when I type fast exactly what's in my head, and when I read again.. Oops, what's this?)*

- *Paying attention to details - include a table of contents (preferably with hyperlinks), a disclaimer, your other offers, write a conclusion, write a thank you page, etc.)*

The most important of all I suppose it's proofreading. Nobody likes errors, especially grammatical ones. I pay a gig on Fiverr who's doing a great job with my books - it's cheap, fast, and she's a really great person to work with. I usually pay $15-$25 for proofreading a document (she charges $5/5,000 words - check her out - outlawsphinx).

#16 - Create an account on Amazon Author Central

Real authors and serious writers use this tool and it's one of the best free promotional tools that Amazon offers. What you need to do is to create a page at http://central.amazon.com and play with the menu. Find your books, write something about yourself and upload a real photo with yourself. In this way, you will assure your customers that you're not a guru hiding behind a computer screen and you're not a robot either - you're a real person and you don't have to be ashamed of who you are.

Your Amazon author central page will help you get in touch with your readers, they will be capable of clicking the follow button, you can connect the page to your blog, Twitter account and so, you can reach more customers. If you have a blog, this will also help you boost up traffic.

I've seen a lot of authors who neglect this page and a lot of other authors who neglect promoting it. Believe it or not this it the most important page that you can have on Amazon. A great description of yourself and having multiple books there will tell people that you're a small authority and they will be more likely to buy your stuff.

#17 - Reward yourself

Work, work, work, but when do we have some fun?

If you were an employee, every year you get a bonus, a reward, you're allowed to go on a vacation and you have other benefits. So why not do these even if you work for yourself?

You see, if you work every day without a single break, without rewarding yourself, you'll end up being depressed and unsatisfied with everything. There are dozens of ways of rewarding yourself:

- *Buy something new*
- *Go to a wellness center*
- *Go to a party or an event*
- *Travel*
- *Meet new people*
- *Spend time with your family*
- *Do anything else unrelated to work*

I'm a big fan of tech, I love having all kinds of gadgets and I also love traveling to all kinds of (safe) destinations. When I made my first $500, I purchase an iPad Mini 4G. When I made another $1,000 I purchased an iPhone 6S (just after it came out, free contract, unlocked) and my new "rewarding" plan is to buy a brand new MacBook PRO 13,3" (for productivity, design, portability and autonomy). I already own a powerful Desktop PC (8-Core CPU, 16GB of RAM, AMD FirePro professional graphics, SSD storage and 2 Full HD 22" monitors) and a decent laptop, but I want a Mac!

I enjoy hiking and I live in Romania, so when I finish a few projects I take 2 days off and go to different places which are also quite, relaxing and cheap.

So, the point is to really do something which you enjoy, do something for yourself to have a good time. After all, that's what life is about - enjoying it and being happy.

#18 - Use the #30,000 rank rule

If you don't know what topic to choose or what books are selling there are a few tricks which you can use to find how if a book's selling. I am pretty sure that you're familiar how Amazon's ranking system works:

#100,000 Paid in Kindle store = ~ 1 sale / day

#50,000 Paid in Kindle store = ~ 3-4 sales/ day

#30,000 Paid in Kindle store = ~ 5-6 sales/day

#10,000 Paid in Kindle store =~ 8-12 sales/ day

Amazon has everything very well organized into categories and subcategories, so what you need to do is to go to the bestsellers list and choose the lowest subcategory. Look at the #1, #40 and #100 of that category and see how that niche is selling - if it's ranked at least #30,000 for #100 position and below #10,000 for the #1st position, then it means that the book is selling well and it's a good niche to get into.

#19 - Publish multiple books on the same topic

I hope you're not the kind of author (or scammer) who writes a book about workouts, one about marketing, one about dog training, a few erotica short novels and other. If you want to become a real author and a real authority in front of others and if you want to convince people that you really know what you're talking about, then you need to focus on 1 niche (or on 2-3 niche which are heavily influenced by your main niche).

For example, I write about online marketing, self-publishing, tips, productivity, self-improvement, growth, etc. but all have one thing in common - they're related to the Laptop Lifestyle.

What you need to do is to start building your own platform - write several books on the same topic and price them differently. When you publish books on similar topic and use different keyword all the time you will surely find people who like what you write about and they will be curious about your other books.

#20 - Find ways to motivate yourself

To be constant in what you're doing, you need to find ways to stay motivated all the time.

What motivates you?

For example, I really love cars, technology and I love traveling to all kinds of (safe) places. I always motivate myself by saying - If I will succeed with my new project this month, I will purchase that. If I finish this other big project, I will take 3 days off and I'll go hiking.

From time to time I like to go to car dealers and ask for a test drive (I recently tested the new Skoda Superb 2015 edition).

There are a lot of other ways which may work for you better. Find them and implement them into your business.

#21 - Diversify your income

Don't put all your eggs in one basket is what they say, and guess what - they're right. It's best to have as many income streams as possible. If writing or self-publishing is your primary source of income, find something else to supplement it. Do it as fast as you can because it's all about your personal financial safety. Here are a few ideas:

Online

- *Start a blog*
- *Start an email list*
- *Start an affiliate marketing campaign*
- *Invest in stocks*

Offline

- *Buy real estate properties and rent them*
- *Buy gold or other precious metal*

I would have one more thing to add on to this subject. Just like Warren Buffet once said, the most important investment that you can make today is in yourself. Constantly invest and improve yourself.

#22 - Create a Perma-Free Book

Every platform and every business has its own free zone. In fact, the most profitable businesses are offering a lot of stuff for free (Google, YouTube, Facebook, Twitter, etc.). Supposing that you have a series of books priced from $0.99 to $2.99, guess what you can do maximize your blog traffic, visibility and even sales of the other books?

A permanently free book is the answer (or the so called perma-free book) on Amazon.

People don't trust a person at the beginning and they are not willing to pay a dime until they get a sample, a free gift, something to prove them that you're a great author.

To set up a perma-free book you have to do 5 things:

1. Upload the book at $0.99.

2. Do not enroll in KDP Select

3. Upload the book somewhere else for free (SmashWords for example).

4. Email Amazon about your free book on other sites and tell them that you want to set your book permanently free.

5. Wait 3 to 6 weeks until Amazon approves your perma-free book.

Tip - don't write lengthy perma-free book - try to write books below 10,000 words.

#23 - Use Countdown Deals

Before reading this tip, please do me a favor and read the KDP Select tip again. If you have a blog, an email list and several books, then consider running Countdown Deals. During a Countdown Deal you can still get a 70% royalty even if you promote your book at $0.99. The whole point here is to get a huge amount of sales within 5 to 7 days to boost your ranking and visibility.

The true magic with Amazon is that sales lead to more sales. The mechanism goes like this - if you make 200 sales in 4 days, your book will be ranked somewhere around #1,000 - #2,000, you will enter the top charts and you will also get additional visibility from "New Hot Releases" and "Customers who also bought this also bought that".

If you have an email list use it to promote these books - simply send an email with your offer and let people know that they're getting a great deal and you would really appreciate their support.

However, don't suffocate your audience with too many offers, try doing Countdown Deals one or twice a month with multiple books at the same time (it's more powerful).

#24 - Use Kindle Matchbook

If you have print editions for your books, then you might want to enroll in Kindle Matchbook - what this does is to offer the Kindle edition or free or discounted (I offer it for free on all my books) to the customers who purchase the print edition. Let's face it, how can we let a customer pay again for the same book after he purchased the print edition (it costs more than double sometimes 10 times more, it takes a lot to deliver and you have to pay shipping and VAT)?

This is a great marketing strategy which I personally use and recommend. The main advantage of this program is to keep your customers up to date with your content - you can update the digital version and send them a message to download it again, but you can't make them purchase the print version of the updated book.

#25 - *Price your books differently*

It's really important to have a catalog with different sizes and prices for your products and thus, for your books. A person who's selling 10 premium books with 200 pages each at $4.99 won't make as much money and won't have as many subscribers as a person who sells 10 books priced and sized differently - 1 book is free (60 pages), 3 books are at $0.99 (60-80 pages), 5 books are at $2.99 (100-120 pages), and 1 book is priced at $4.99.

Customers initially get the free copy. They have the chance to learn more about your writing style and about you. If they like your free book, they will buy your $0.99 books. If you helped them out and answered to their questions or you entertained them (fiction), then they will also purchase the $2.99 and $3.99 books.

Having 10 books at the same price will still bring you money but people will avoid purchasing before knowing you. I would do the same.

#26 - *Constantly improve yourself*

You will see how your skills improve only after you look back after several months what you've written previously and you'll think "man, I sucked at the beginning". You see, this is basically the main purpose of life - to grow and to constantly improve, adapt and change ourselves.

The same principle is applied here - if you want to grow, to be successful, to make money, and to become an authority, then you need to find ways (on your own) to improve your writing style, vocabulary, grammar, humor, techniques, marketing strategies, how to be more productive, etc.

I learned a lot of new things in 1 year of self-publishing and I'm proud to say that every single day I did something for the growth of this business.

#27 - Share your work on Social Media

Even if you hate social media (like I do), keep in mind that your business depends on it. Facebook, Twitter, LinkedIn, etc. have great advertising services and you can grow your email list and thus, you can make more sales which lead to more money and more visibility.

Create accounts where you can and try to keep all of them up to date by constantly adding news/posts and of course, offers or deals.

On social media you can interact with other authors or self-publishers just like you and share ideas.

I've used Facebook ads and it's one of the best tool for growing and email list.

#28 - Hire a VA

We can't do everything on our own. We need someone to help us all the time - an assistant, employers, managers, etc. Even online businesses require some help so you can speed everything up.

Go to Upwork, Freelancer or Fiverr to hire someone to help you out with the easy (time consuming) tasks - cover creation, proofreading, illustrating, formatting, editing, video editing, audio editing, content SEO optimizing, etc.

On top of all of these, you can hire a virtual assistant (your personal manager) to manage all those easy tasks and payments. Most of the successful businesses have their trained personal (or virtual) assistants.

Remember, time is money, so don't waste it. Make everything you can to outsource easy tasks and focus on your main activities - write your bokos, manage your blog, come up with new ideas, relax, etc.

#29 - Set goals

Setting goals is one of the key features for any business. I wouldn't have made any money or had any success with my business if I didn't do it. Track your performance, set weekly, monthly, yearly and long term (+10 years) goals.

In other words, organize your activity, budget and capabilities. Merge them all together and start running towards your dreams and goals. Some of them will be easy to achieve, some of them realizable and some of them will be accomplished only with a lot of effort and luck. Try not to overwhelm yourself with unrealistic goals, especially at the beginning.

#30 - Co-author books

Writing a book together with another author (or authors) is a great strategy. The principle is very simple:

If an author has 20,000 subscribers, a blog, a free gift and 15 books and another author has 15,000 subscribers, a blog, a free gift and 20 books, when they co-author a book, they can both include their offers, gifts and links to their blog and there comes the magic - you will boost the book's sales from both parties. If you sell 10% from those 20,000 and 10% from those 15,000 you will almost double the sales.

As I said previously, on Amazon sales lead to more sales, so your ranking will skyrocket and you will make even more money. It's true that you're splitting profits with the other author(s), but it's much more effective and subscribers who liked an author, will also check your stuff too, so you will make additional sales indirectly.

It's really great to co-author a few books, they shouldn't be missing from your offer.

#31 - Help others

If there's any lesson for those who are seeking (legit) success, that lesson is to help others without asking something in return. Adding value to what you do and helping others will help you out with everything you do.

When you do someone a favor without asking for something in return, they will come back for more when they need to. If this happens even more often, then people will also help you out with your business (buy your products, subscribe, give you a thumbs up, leave a nice comment, share your work, they will thank you, etc.)

Let's apply this principle to an online business.

If you're looking on the Internet to solve a problem (ex: which is the perfect laptop for $500; how to build an email list fast?; how to overcome anxiety?) and you offer them guidance (a post, an offer, a video, an email), they will think exactly like this "Hmm... this guy has great stuff, maybe I should subscribe for updates". Then, by following you, people will learn more, you will add even more value to them and eventually they will become your permanent customers.

I have done that myself. There are people on the Internet (some of my idols) from whom I learned life changing ways of making money online, I learned dozens of new things for which I am grateful today. People to whom I subscribed and followed on the long term made me buy their products naturally and that's because they added value.

Just add value to what you do and you won't regret it!

#32 - Sign up to multiple forums

This tip is available for any kind of niche and for any type of bloggers. By joining forums and starting discussion or by adding comments to other existing threads will give you traffic and visibility. It's great to do this every week, especially for authority blogs (from your niche) as they remain there and people will always find you (your comments/threads remain there permanently).

Regarding self-publishing, the best 2 forums where you can promote your books, blog, etc. are Kboards and Warriorforum.

#33 - Publish on other platforms

Amazon is the leading platform when it comes to selling books, but it's not recommended to focus just on Amazon (or to put all your eggs in one basket). When you enroll in KDP Select, they are forcing you to sell your book exclusively on Kindle. At the beginning it's really great. When you don't have any background in the industry, KDP Select is the best option, the other platforms won't give you Amazon's visibility and traffic.

At some point, you will make money and become successful. When you do that, you need to take into consideration all the tips from this booklet (create an email list, a blog, multiple books on the same niche, a perma-free book, etc.). Remember the tip where I said that it's best to have a variety of prices and sizes? Well, that includes uploading a few books on other platforms too. Upload on all the other platforms (where you're accepted) a perma-free book (for traffic and more visibility), a bargain $0.99 book and $2.99 or even $4.99 books.

We will never know what happens with Amazon in the next 10 years, so the wise thing to do is to try to expand where we can.

Other Books By Ryan Stevens

Amazon Associates Affiliate Program

Learn what Affiliate Marketing is, how it is done and how you can start your own.

[$0.99 Book] - Online Startup – How To Make Money Online Even When You Don't Have Any

Most startups require money, so to initially make money, start from the bottom. Use the information within this book and use the simplest method to make money online even today.

[$0.99 Book] - CreateSpace For Independent Self-Publishers

Nowadays, people prefer to buy digital eBooks instead of physical ones because it's faster, cheaper, environmentally friendly, and you theoretically have unlimited stock. However, there still are people who prefer physical books and they pay for them even though they're more expensive. You can publish just on CreateSpace or you can publish on both Kindle and CreateSpace (I recommend doing both).

Evernote In 90 Minutes Or Less

Not only can you find unlimited ways of using this app for de-cluttering and organizing your life, but while you do that, developers will also find more ways to improve it and add more features to it.

Express Book Launch

Launching a book on Amazon is a complex strategy that takes months to be correctly understood. For most authors on Amazon, this has been the most challenging process of the business.

Entrepreneur Enhanced

You don't have to be an expert, and you don't have to be perfect in what you do; you only need to be committed to what you do. You have to always push and move on, no matter what happens. Nobody said that it will be easy to become an entrepreneur. "Now" is the right time to get started.

Kindle Publishing PRO

Unlike other books that regurgitate the same information because they're written by inexperienced publishers, this guide will give you the key information from an author who has done it time and time again. Just a few years ago, the idea of publishing a book was far out of reach for most everyone, but with the help of this giant online marketplace, you can quickly and safely publish your own book and make a profit!

More will come up soon, sign up to my newsletter for offers at $0.99 or FREE books – *http://entrepreneurenhanced.com*

Write a review

I am constantly improving my books and my work and I am trying to deliver my readers the best quality information. To improve my work and myself as a human being, I need reviews to know where I am wrong or where I have made mistakes.

Remember, there is no such thing as a perfect book, it needs updates all the time, especially if it's digital.

If this book has been useful to you, please write a review with all your thoughts, it won't take more than 1 minute.

If you didn't like something from this book, please contact me and I will try to solve your problem.

Thank you,

Ryan